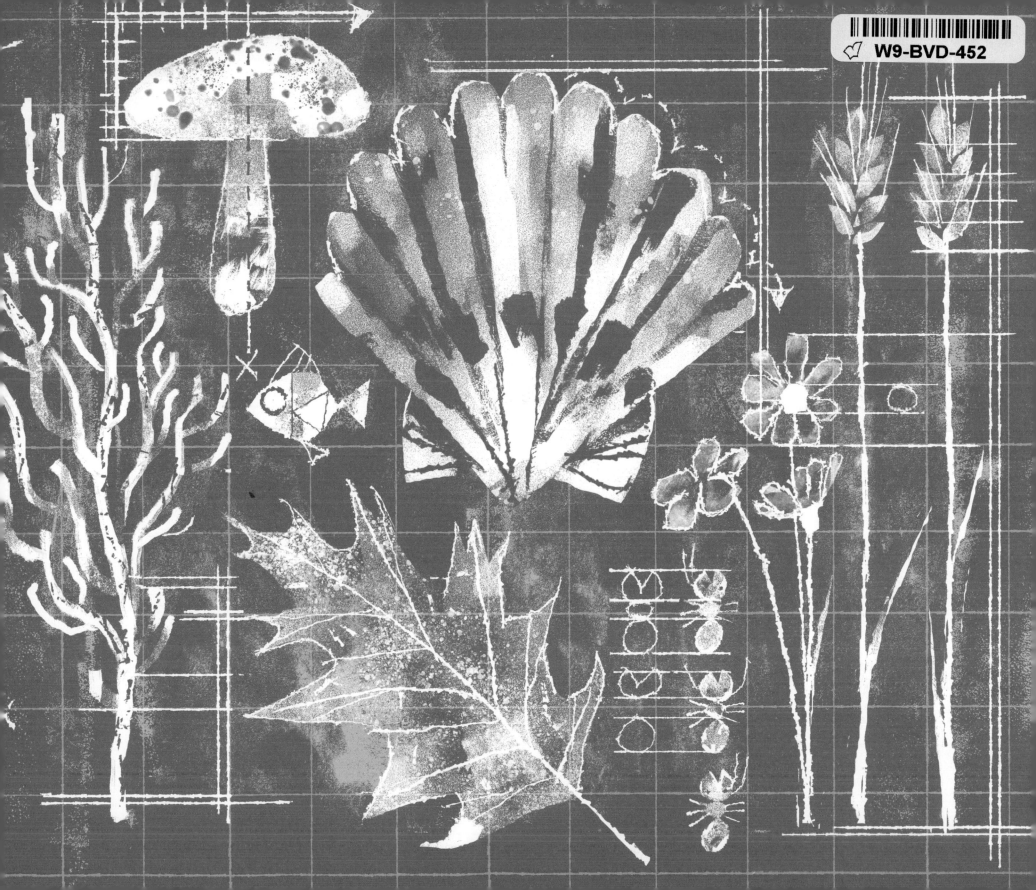

For Zoey Azadan,
with love and hope for the wonderful life
she will design and build—A. C.

To Caleb and Eliana—C. S.

BEACH LANE BOOKS
An imprint of Simon & Schuster Children's Publishing Division
1230 Avenue of the Americas, New York, New York 10020
Text © 2021 by Amy Cherrix
Illustrations © 2021 by Chris Sasaki
Book design by Lauren Rille © 2021 by Simon & Schuster, Inc.
All rights reserved, including the right of reproduction in whole or in part in any form.
BEACH LANE BOOKS is a trademark of Simon & Schuster, Inc.
For information about special discounts for bulk purchases, please contact Simon & Schuster Special Sales
at 1-866-506-1949 or business@simonandschuster.com.
The Simon & Schuster Speakers Bureau can bring authors to your live event. For more information or to book an event,
contact the Simon & Schuster Speakers Bureau at 1-866-248-3049 or visit our website at www.simonspeakers.com.
The text for this book was set in Archer.
The illustrations for this book were rendered digitally.
Manufactured in China
0621 SCP
First Edition
10 9 8 7 6 5 4 3 2 1
Library of Congress Cataloging-in-Publication Data • Names: Cherrix, Amy E., author. | Sasaki, Chris (Illustrator), illustrator. • Title: Animal architects /
Amy Cherrix ; illustrated by Chris Sasaki. • Description: New York : Beach Lane Books, [2021] | Audience: Ages 3–8 | Audience: Grades 2–3 | Summary:
"Did you know the natural world is a construction zone? Amazing animals all over the world are building all kinds of structures every single day. This
fascinating, fact-filled book will captivate young scientists and naturalists and have them looking out for animal construction projects happening in their
own backyards!"—Provided by publisher. • Identifiers: LCCN 2020052204 (print) | LCCN 2020052205 (ebook) | ISBN 9781534456259 (hardcover) | ISBN
9781534456266 (ebook) • Subjects: LCSH: Animals—Habitations—Juvenile literature. | Animal behavior—Juvenile literature. • Classification: LCC QL756
.C4838 2021 (print) | LCC QL756 (ebook) | DDC 591.56/4—dc23 • LC record available at https://lccn.loc.gov/2020052204 • LC ebook record available at
https://lccn.loc.gov/2020052205

# ANIMAL ARCHITECTS

written by
**AMY CHERRIX**

illustrated by
**CHRIS SASAKI**

Beach Lane Books • New York  London  Toronto  Sydney  New Delhi

**D**id you know the natural world is a construction zone? Whether they are large or small, in the ocean or on land, animals are amazing architects!

Imagine working on a project for 10,000 years. That's what this coral has been doing. The tiny larvae have been building reefs for what feels like forever to create . . .

. . . this undersea city!

Teeming with life, the Great Barrier Reef in Australia is the world's largest living structure. It spans an area of 133,000 square miles. It's even visible from outer space.

The trapdoor spider covers the entrance
to its ground burrow with a door built of
silken thread. Long strands fan out from
the burrow across the ground. Now, to wait
for its next victim . . .

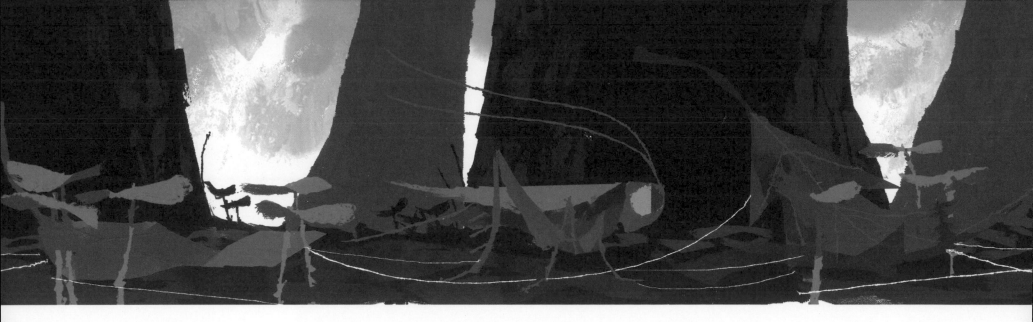

When an unsuspecting insect steps on the spider-silk strands,
the burrow vibrates like a silent doorbell.

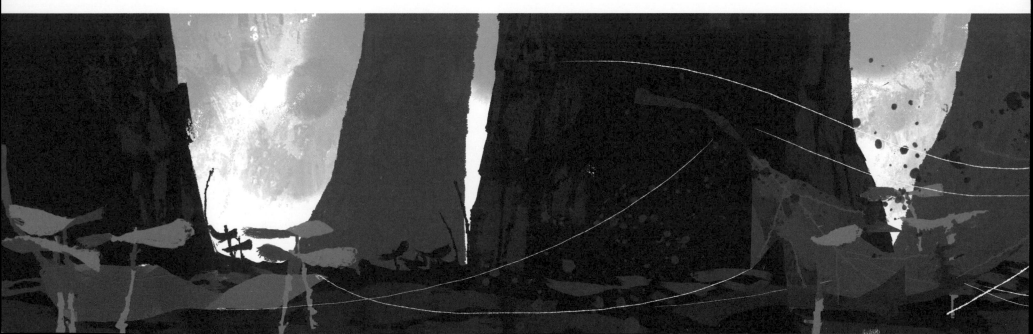

*WHOOSH!* The hungry spider springs
from behind its tricky trapdoor! At last, a delicious snack.

For several days, a male satin bowerbird gathers
grasses and tiny twigs, shaping them into a hut
or an upside-down arch, called a bower.

Soon it's time . . .

. . . to decorate!

In order to attract a mate, his bower must be beautiful. He carefully places matching piles of colorful petals and shiny shells at the bower's entrance. *Churr! Churr!* The satin bowerbird calls. Who will be the first guest?

This tiny ant is one mighty mover. The load
of dirt she hauls from the anthill weighs more
than her body! It's a good thing she's not alone.
Beneath the anthill, millions
more female worker ants
are constructing . . .

. . . a colony.

Deep in their underground home, the ants dig
a roller-coaster network of tunnels and trails.
Together, these industrious insects can remove
2,205 pounds of earth per year.

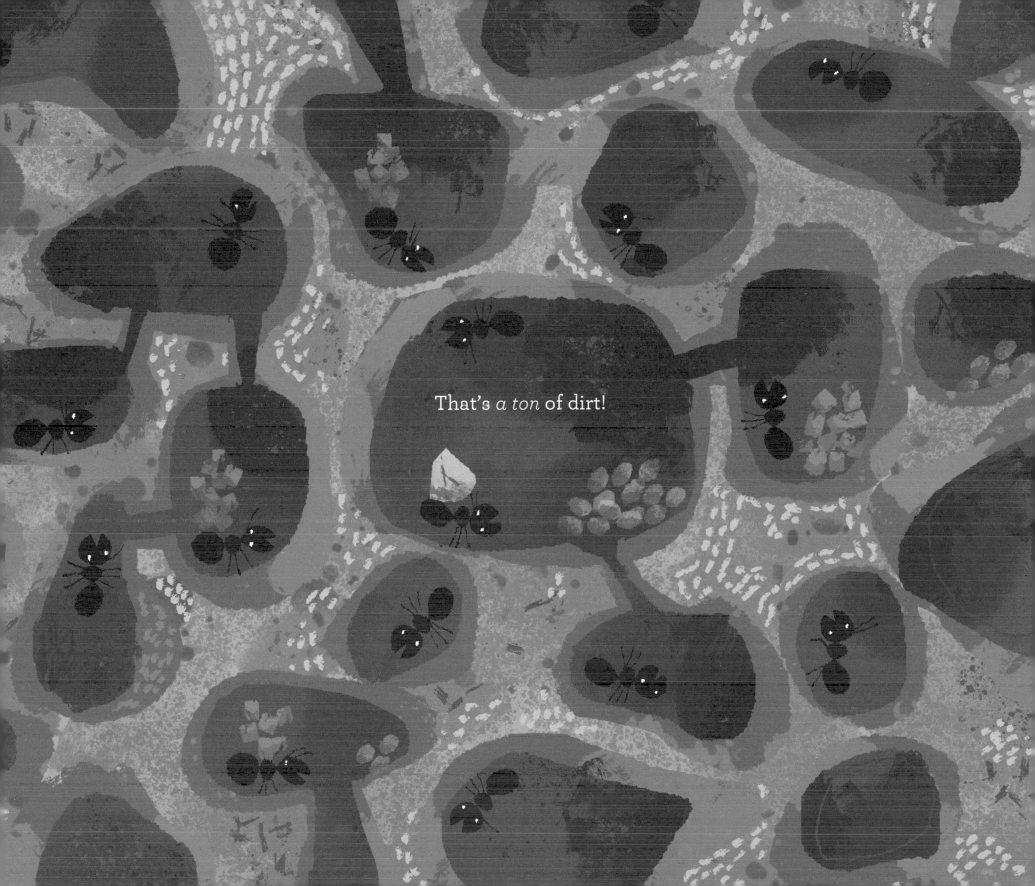

That's *a ton* of dirt!

A pair of gentoo penguins combs an Antarctic beach collecting pebbles. Soon the female will lay eggs. There's no time to waste.

She needs . . .

. . . a nest.

The busy penguins pile the pebbles into a round
mound. They fill it with feathers  and soft moss.

When the mother penguin is ready, she settles down and lays her eggs in a palace of pebbles.

Black-tailed prairie dogs are expert diggers. Their underground home, called a burrow, is a twisty highway of tunnels, which includes chambers for sleeping, eating, and pooping.

As the burrow expands it becomes . . .

. . . a dog town.

The largest recorded prairie dog town
spanned 25,000 square miles and housed as
many as 400 million prairie dogs!

Cathedral termites mix dirt with saliva
and roll it into bricks to build their home.

As the bricks stack up, a tower nearly thirty feet tall rises from the desert floor to become . . .

. . . a termite mound.

How do millions of these wee workers keep cool in their high-rise home? The unique shape of the mound stores heat during the day and releases it at night. The termites live in a solar-powered tower.

The carrier snail is a clever crafter. Its body releases a sticky goo, like glue. Using its muscular foot, the snail attaches nearby shells to its own shell to create . . .

. . . body armor.

The extra spiky shell might help
disguise the carrier snail and
discourage hungry predators in
search of a soft seafood supper.

A busy honeybee sips nectar from a blossom.
Once it's full of flower juice, the bee buzzes
home to help build . . .

. . . a hive.

Inside, the flower nectar is passed along
to more bees, who turn it into honey.
They mix the sweet syrup into beeswax.
The bees chew the wax and it hardens
into glue to shape the hive. Teamwork and
beeswax hold the honeybees' home together.

A beaver is nature's lumberjack. It can gnaw through a tall tree in just three minutes!

Next, it floats the heavy log
through the water to build . . .

. . . a beaver dam.

Together, the male and female beavers push heavy rocks into place. They pack mud with their paws.

When the beaver dam is complete, they have created
a safe place for their family to live and a brand-new
pond that every animal in the forest will enjoy.

The harvest mouse is no bigger than your thumb. But her long, strong tail holds her in place between thick grass stalks while she works.

With her sharp teeth, the harvest mouse
tears the grasses into strips and gathers them
between her paws. She begins weaving a tiny
bead. In two days' time, the bead grows bigger
and eventually becomes . . .

. . . a mouse house.

A tennis-ball-sized nest, safely
suspended in a forest of reeds.

Everywhere you look, animal architects are hard at work, designing, building, and decorating their amazing animal kingdom.

## SELECTED SOURCES

**Books**

Arndt, Ingo. *Animal Architecture*. New York: Abrams, 2014.

Atkinson, Sam et al., eds. *Explanatorium of Nature*. New York: DK Publishing, 2017.

Jenkins, Steve. *The Animal Book*. New York: Houghton Mifflin Harcourt, 2013.

**Other Media**

Kaufman, Fred, producer. *Nature*. Season 32, episode 17, "Leave It to Beavers." May 14, 2014. "How Beavers Build Dams."
Video clip, 2:32. www.pbs.org/wnet/nature/leave-it-to-beavers-video-how-beavers-build-dams/8847/

Lindholm, Jane, and Melody Bodette. "How Do Bees Make Honey and Why Do They Sting?" August, 18, 2017.
www.vpr.org/post/how-do-bees-make-honey-and-why-do-they-sting#stream/0

Morell, Virginia. "Build It (and They Will Come)." *National Geographic*, July 2010.
www.nationalgeographic.com/magazine/2010/07/bowerbirds/#

National Geographic. "Gentoo Penguin." www.nationalgeographic.com/animals/birds/g/gentoo-penguin/

National Geographic. "Prairie Dog." www.nationalgeographic.com/animals/mammals/group/prairie-dogs/

National Oceanic and Atmospheric Administration. "How Do Coral Reefs Form?"
https://oceanservice.noaa.gov/education/tutorial_corals/coral04_reefs.html

National Oceanic and Atmospheric Administration. "What Is the Great Barrier Reef?"
https://oceanservice.noaa.gov/facts/gbrlargeststructure.html

Salisbury, Mike, dir. *Life in the Undergrowth*. Episode 3, "The Silk Spinners." Presented by David Attenborough.
BBC, 2005.

Shipman, Matt. "How Do Bees Make Honey? (It's Not Just Bee Barf)," NC State University News, June 19, 2013.
news.ncsu.edu/2013/06/how-do-bees-make-honey/

Zielinski, Sarah. "Tiny Ants Move a Ton of Soil." *Science News*, July 20, 2016.
https://www.sciencenews.org/blog/wild-things/tiny-ants-move-ton-soil